W9-DAV-067

1. The Danube embankment, Buda
71. The Danube with the building of the Parliament

Photographs by
Demeter Balla: 20, 24
Imre Benkő: 43, 52
Lóránt Bérczi: 16, 47, 48, 66
László Csigó: 45, 55, 60–63
Lajos Czeizing: 41, 50, 51
Endre Domonkos: 49
János Eifert: 12, 13, 15, 22, 23, 46
László Gyarmati: 2–4, 64, 65
Károly Hemző: 6, 7, 8, 18, 25, 30, 42, 53, 57, 67, 68
Tibor Inkey: 36, 38
Rudolf Járai: 44
Péter Korniss: 56
Sándor Kovács: 9, 40
Lajos Köteles: 29
József Szabó: 10, 54, 58
Zsolt Szabóky: 21, 69, 70
Károly Szelényi: 5, 11
László Szelényi: 14, 27
János Szerencsés: 26, 28
Gyula Tahin: 17, 19, 31–35, 37, 39, 59
András Tokaji: 71 (back)
György Wessely 1 (cover)

Fourth edition

Translated by Judith E. Sollosy
Design by Erzsébet Szabados
Cover design by Róbert Eszes

© Péter Dobai, 1980
ISBN 963 13 1970 9
Printed in Hungary, 1984
Kner Printing House, Dürer Workshop, Békéscsaba
CO 2263–h–8486

An old port, an old haven, an old royal free borough whose rich past reaches back to the distant centuries of the Roman Empire, Budapest lies on two banks of the Danube, the most beautiful river in Europe. And although this city is located deep within the heart of Europe, the Danube connects it, like so many others, with the sea. Originally, Budapest was three separate towns—Óbuda, Buda and Pest, which were united in 1872, and which, through the years, became a truly major capital city. But even before the Romans came, the caves of Buda, its forests rich in game and vegetation, the thermal springs of its gently rolling hills sloping down to the Danube attracted many settlers. Later the Roman legions camped by the Danube, on the site of today's Óbuda, and soon their camp grounds developed into Aquincum, the capital of the province of Lower Pannonia. Its massive walls, however, were razed to the ground by the resurgent waves of the Great Migrations and were consequently buried under the mud of Danubian floods. Luckily, the 20th century has uncovered the ancient routes and atriums, the foundations of the Roman castrums, so that today Aquincum stands on the bank of the Danube as a song of praise to the past. The ruins of that most important Roman-age establishment, the amphitheatre, whose arena was filled over a thousand years ago by the motley tents of the conquering Magyars, also stand today as a robust reminder of Antique culture. During the Middle Ages, the status of Buda as a city grew: it won the rights of a port and of holding regional fairs from the kings. In the wake of the terrible ravages of the Mongol Invasion, the construction of the Castle of Buda (1247) was begun, whose stormy history has defined the lives and fates of the merchants, craftsmen, grape-growers

and fruit merchants who settled behind its bastions and below its walls in increasingly greater numbers. However, after a rich Renaissance flowering, the city and country fell under Turkish rule for a hundred and fifty years, and was wrenched out of the mainstream of European development. The united Christian armies succeeded in recapturing the Castle only in 1686, at the time of the decline of the Turkish empire. Most of the medieval houses perished during the long siege, and afterwards, the district took on its baroque appearance which still characterizes it today. The two towns of Buda and Pest were united in the energetic and optimistic 19th century, the age of the steamship and the railway, a marriage as much hallmarked by the dynamic appearance of new bridges spanning the Danube as by the new, monumental cityscape. From all parts of the country and beyond, the main thoroughfares and railways converged on the new city.

Yet Budapest had to undergo another rebirth after the Second World War. In the spring of 1945, when the last canons had fallen silent, Budapest was a city of the homeless and of dismal ruins, a city without bridges. But it was rebuilt once more—a triumph of determination over the passion for destruction. Today the bridges, those lovely bridges of Pest and Buda, arch over the river once again, and new districts, new housing estates bear witness to peace. Along all great rivers, great cities rise; Budapest is the city of the Danube, of its bridges and islands, indivisible from it, living and breathing along with its heaving waters which surge towards the south. Indeed, Budapest's most breathtaking monument is the Danube itself. No architect or stone-cutter has ever conceived a more magnificent edifice than this 'edifice' of water which had stood here long before man ever settled its shores, and whose water had

given sustenance and a means of transportation to a long row of successive generations. Budapest's most beautiful and best-known buildings, old and new alike, were all built on the banks of the Danube or overlooking its waters from the surrounding hillsides. On its eastern bank, in Pest, stand the building of the Parliament, the Hungarian Academy of Sciences, a row of modern luxury hotels, the Inner City Parish Church whose history goes back to the Middle Ages, and the neo-Renaissance edifice of the Karl Marx University of Economics. In Buda, on the western bank of the river, lie the old thermal baths and modern pools, the villas on Rózsadomb (Rose Hill), the famed Fishermen's Bastion, the Matthias Church, the Hilton Hotel and the Royal Palace on Castle Hill, the Citadella, the impressive Secessionist Gellért Hotel and Baths on Gellért Hill, and further to the south, the University of Technology, and many apartment and public buildings—all facing the Danube, the mighty river which carries the legend of Budapest down to the sea.

In fact, the most pleasant way of approaching Budapest is by boat on the Danube. On the way from up north, the passangers can see the Basilica rising high above the town of Esztergom, the ruins of the royal castle of Visegrád, and the most breathtaking sight of all, the Danube Bend, followed by the cathedral of Vác and the towers of this bishop's town—and along the banks, there stand a gentle chain of hills, Szentendre's colourful rooftops with their touch of the Mediterranean. Drifting past dark green, seemingly deserted islands, the traveller will then see the Roman Banks, a popular beach with boathouses and rows of poplars, and finally, the misty silhouettes of the towers and domes of Budapest itself.

The city has two hearts: Buda on its hills and Pest on its plains.

Someone looking down at Budapest from Gellért Hill, the Fishermen's Bastion or the lookout tower of János Hill sees *one* city, but he who gets to know Budapest learns to love *two* towns. Buda lies on the heights, the sides and terraces of the hills and mountains, the *home* of the past. Facing it from the east is Pest, much larger than Buda in territory, with its new housing projects seemingly hovering over the flat, distant horizon and its massive industrial districts on the outskirts. In contrast to the intimacy of romantic, baroque-style Buda, its dimensions are truly on a grand scale. In fact, Pest too is old, ancient, and has retained vestiges of this past, though not as openly as Buda. The former town walls and gates, the marble remains of ancient, dried-out wells can still be seen, though, in the courtyards and firewalls of the Inner City, sometimes in quite good condition. As long as this city stands, Buda will always remain the royal city,

and Pest the bourgeois town, the alliance of the two blessed by the bridges over the Danube. Buda has retained the historical and architectural monuments due to a royal seat—the Castle, forts, palaces, monasteries and churches that belong to the past. With its larger proportions, Pest bears the stamps of bourgeois virtues and of conscious city planning. Its boulevards, avenues and roundabouts belong to the age of industrial development. Buda offers a more picturesque sight, while Pest is more practical and massive. Buda's rich and effective, sometimes modest architectural remains force man to accomodate himself to past centuries, while the fate of Pest is dictated by the present. Though Pest has long ago gained ascendancy with its two operas, many theatres, sports stadiums and academies of the fine and performing arts, of the humanities and sciences, Buda has kept the best of itself: historical monuments which, for us today, are

becoming more and more precious,
and the prerogative of seigniority
with its more ancient walls and
their hidden secrets, its prerogative
of a sense of painful recall and
of nostalgia.

A man walking around Budapest
becomes acquainted with a different
city in Buda, and a different city
in Pest. But his walk in either
part of the capital takes him along
the banks of the same river, which
finally unites Buda and Pest into the
one and only Budapest. Whether
he strolls in the Castle District or
among the medieval and baroque
houses of Buda, captivated by their
seemingly purposeless archways,
perhaps imagining himself in
another century for one illogical
instant; whether he walks through
the domed Turkish baths below
the Castle or wanders around the
streets of Pest, where past and
present merge and vie for
prominence, he is enjoying the sights
of an unforgettable city, one he
will want to visit again and again,
to walk through its Castle area, its
Gellért Hill, and to climb the
lookout towers on the hills of Buda,
from where he can see the great
semicircles formed by Buda and
Pest, with the Danube, this
historical equator of East and West
between them.

Péter Dobai

2–4 Buda as seen from Pest
5 The Castle District
seen from Gellért Hill ▷

6 Roman tombstone in Aquincum
7 Aquincum:
ruins of the civilian town
8 Turkish tombstones on Castle Hill

9 The southern Round Bastion
of Buda Castle
10 The Mace Tower

11 The Royal Castle of Buda
12 The Matthias Fountain
in the courtyard of the Castle

13 Detail of one of the Castle courtyards

14–15 The Hungarian National Gallery in the Castle

16 The Gothic Hall of the Castle

17 Bécsikapu Square
18 The Hilton Hotel

19 King Matthias's monument
on the Gothic tower of St. Nicholas'
Church
20 Terrace of the Hilton Hotel

21 The Fishermen's Bastion
with the Parliament building
in the background ▷

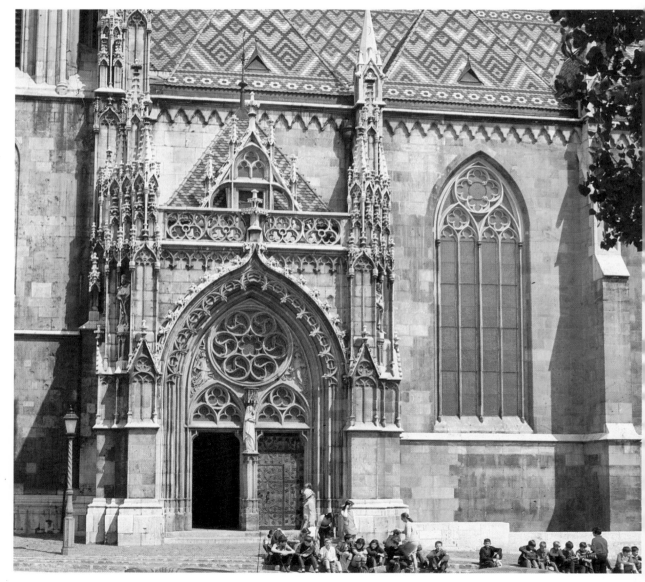

◁ 22–25 Matthias Church in the
Castle District

26 Országház Street
27 The old Town Hall of Buda
on Szentháromság Square
28 Courtyard of the Red Hedgehog
Inn (3. Hess András Square)

29 Front door of 25 Fortuna Street
30 Gothic niches in the gateway
of 13 Tárnok Street
31 Gothic niches, 32 Úri Street
32 Courtyard of the house at 13
Dísz Square

33 6 Bécsikapu Square
34 14–16 Tárnok Street
35 12–14 Fortuna Street
36 Dárda Street

37 Biedermeier house with
corner turret on the corner of Fő
and Pala Streets
38 Detail of the Tabán area
on Gellért Hill

39 Gül Baba street in Buda
40 Rococo house on Batthyány
Square

◁ 41 The Chain Bridge with
Margaret Bridge and Margaret
Island in the background

42 Tibor Vilt's statue
of the 19th-century dramatist
Imre Madách on Margaret Island
43 Children playing on Margaret
Island

44 The Island in autumn ▷

48 The Fountain of the Nereids
in front of the Franciscan Church
49 Kossuth Lajos Street, a main
thoroughfare of Pest

53 The Danubius Fountain
on Engels Square
54 Vörösmarty Square

55 Façade of the building
at 3 Martinelli Square
56 Petőfi Sándor Street

◁ 57 Kígyó Street
◁ 58 Felszabadulás Square seen
from the Paris Arcades

59 Rákóczi Street
60–62 Buildings constructed
at the turn of the century
in Rákóczi Street
and József Boulevard

63 Népköztársaság Avenue
64 Art nouveau building
in Ajtósi Dürer Road

65 Detail of the Millennial
Monument in Hősök tere (Heroes'
Square)
66 Hősök tere

67 Miklós Ligeti's statue of
Anonymus, the chronicler of King
Béla III (13th century)
68 The Pond in City Park
with Vajdahunyad Castle
in the background

69 The Danube
with the Liberty Bridge ▷

70 The Parliament building seen from Castle Hill